BRIAN PATTEN

armada

Flamingo
An Imprint of HarperCollinsPublishers

Flamingo
An Imprint of HarperCollins*Publishers*
77–85 Fulham Palace Road,
Hammersmith, London w6 8jb

A Paperback Original 1996
1 3 5 7 9 8 6 4 2

First published in Great Britain by
HarperCollins*Publishers* 1996

A catalogue record for this book
is available from the British Library

ISBN 0 00 665039 8

Set in Bembo by
Rowland Phototypesetting Ltd,
Bury St Edmunds, Suffolk

Printed in Great Britain by
Caledonian International Book Manufacturing Ltd, Glasgow

For my mother, Irene Stella Bevan

ACKNOWLEDGEMENTS

The Minister for Exams was first published in The Guardian newspaper; *So Many Different Lengths of Time*, based on six lines from a poem by Pablo Neruda translated by Lucia Graves, was first published in The New Statesman, as was *Inessential Things*; *Tina's Flight* was written for a memorial reading for the poet Tina Faulkner; *Garden Lore* was first published in The Sunday Telegraph Magazine. Many of the poems first found a public at poetry readings, and my thanks are due to the people who arranged the readings and the many who have supported them.

All the plans you made you put aside so long
That even on the best a mildew formed,
And as the years passed
You clung to old contracts though they'd lapsed,
And in the narrow resolutions of the past
You were stuck although
There was so much you longed to do.
And now three-quarters through what time is left
You realize you have hardly scratched
The surface of the world;
So much has been left undone it appals,
And there is so little time before a greater darkness calls.

CONTENTS

1 the armada

2 between harbours

3 inessential things

I

the armada

Cinders

You never went to a ball, ever.
In all your years sweeping kitchens
No fairy godmother appeared, never.

Poor, poor sweetheart,
This rough white cloth, fresh from the hospital laundry,
Is the only theatre-gown you've ever worn.

No make-up. Hair matted with sweat.
The drip beside your bed discontinued.
Life was never a fairy-tale.

Cinders soon.

The Armada

Long long ago
when everything I was told was believable
and the little I knew was less limited than now,
I stretched belly down on the grass beside a pond
and to the far bank launched a child's armada.
    A broken fortress of twigs,
the paper-tissue sails of galleons,
the waterlogged branches of submarines –
all came to ruin and were on flame
in that dusk-red pond.
And you, mother, stood behind me,
impatient to be going,
old at twenty-three, alone,
thin overcoat flapping.
    How closely the past shadows us.
In a hospital a mile or so from that pond
I kneel beside your bed and, closing my eyes,
reach out across forty years to touch once more
that pond's cool surface,
and it is your cool skin I'm touching;
for as on a pond a child's paper boat
was blown out of reach
by the smallest gust of wind,
so too have you been blown out of reach

by the smallest whisper of death,
and a childhood memory is sharpened,
and the heart burns as that armada burnt,
long, long ago.

The Betrayal

By the time I got to where I had no intention of going
Half a lifetime had passed.
I'd sleepwalked so long. While I dozed
Houses outside which gas-lamps had spluttered
Were pulled down and replaced,
And my background was wiped from the face of the earth.

There was so much I ought to have recorded,
So many lives that have vanished –
Families, neighbours; people whose pockets
Were worn thin by hope. They were
The loose change history spent without caring.
Now they have become the air I breathe,
Not to have marked their passing seems such a betrayal.

Other things caught my attention:
A caterpillar climbing a tree in a playground,
A butterfly resting on a doorknob.
And my grandmother's hands!
Though I saw those poor, sleeping hands
Opening and closing like talons,
I did not see the grief they were grasping.
The seed of my long alienation from those I loved
Was wrapped in daydreams.

Something I've never been able to pinpoint
Led me away from the blood I ought to have recorded.
I search my history for reasons, for omens. But what use now
Zodiacs, or fabulous and complicated charts
Offered up by fly-brained astrologers?
What use now supplications?

In the clouds' entrails I constantly failed
To read the true nature of my betrayal.
What those who shaped me could not articulate
Still howls for recognition as a century closes,
And their homes are pulled down and replaced,
And their backgrounds are wiped from the face of the earth.

The Eavesdropper

From my vantage point on the top stair
of a house that no longer exists,
I sat like a cabin boy who listens in secret
to the crew of a great, creaking ship,
and eavesdropped on the adults below me.
A dial searched through the static
of radio wavelengths. Band music.
A fug of voices. Light. Comfort.
Soporific sounds cotton-wrapped the heart
and sent me, a little spy, sleepwards.

I do not know what happened while I slept,
Nor how long I slept. I cannot say.
But waking, I peered down into darkness.
No voices. Silence. In a blink it seemed
Familiar objects had become antiquated.
Whatever secrets I had hoped to uncover
were never uncovered, and now
are covered by gravestones or burnt to ashes.

I cannot blame that child his lack of attention.
He would have understood their secrets
no more than I can understand why, once again,
I attempt to eavesdrop on them,
and move down, stair by stair, towards them.

Echoes

With arthritic hands and red-varnished nails
She drags herself up the wooden stairs,
The frightening heartbeat of the house
Is made by her iron callipers.
The bomb-crushed legs, the bolted bones,
The hands that scrape like talons on the stairs,
The damned-up pain, the hate, the grief;
The soul crushed by iron callipers.

Beneath grey government-issue blankets I
Lie in a makeshift bed, feigning sleep.
Five years old. I hear her weep
As she drags herself up the wooden stairs.
Like a ball and chain her iron callipers.

She rejects all help, all love as I
In later years will learn to do.
Five years old. I cower from her authority.
Clunk. Clunk. Clunk.
The sound echoes through my history,
And imprisons me.

Neighbourhood Watch

This street has grown stale.
The house in which the old Jamaican lived
has given up the will to dance.
The young lawyer and his lovely wife
have dug up his garden. Gone now
the remnants of his failed experiments –
the exotic blooms that never quite happened,
the plants that, like him, never wholly took root.

One by one the souls of these houses and their tenants
have been undone by the fingers of bankers.
Among the debris where the religious lady wept
now only a sprinkler weeps. Those refugees from
the way things are supposed to be – the mysterious Pole,
the Italian students, the immaculate prostitute –
all gone from number seven.

Behind the window of number forty
nothing moves any more. How suddenly
that house lost its tongue! Within a year of each other
the old maids who lived there
donated their observations to the grave.
Like them, this street has grown secretive.

Glimpsed behind car windows bored children
are ferried back and forth, and are eaten up by doors.
Neighbours slip from memory, all their battles
and secret torments melting so effortlessly away.
Rooms are repainted, lavish curtains appear in windows.
This street has suddenly grown staid.
On the wall of the alcoholic playwright's house
a blue plaque has sealed its fate. Alarm bells ring
too late to be of use. The street's soul, stolen long ago.

Inattention

A child sitting on a doorstep looks up from his book.
In the room behind him a woman is writing a letter.
On the waste land across the street from him
a gasometer casts its shadow over a solitary lilac.

Like a little animal grazing over grass
he has been grazing over words,
stopping at the unfamiliar, the wondrous.
Over and over, as if it were a spell, he repeats the word *cargo*.

Out on an ocean phosphite clings to rusting propellers,
whales rise like islands, rain falls into nothing.
The shadow from the gasometer creeps beyond the lilac,
over the bindweed, the sweet-scented camomiles, the stray
     thistles.

And now the child has abandoned his book.
He has become the captain of a great ship and its cargo of
     treasure.
Sailors who've lost their sight report to him
on how the stars have vanished.

In the house behind him a woman is packing belongings.
Another book, an encyclopedia of regrets, is banished to its
    own space.
The shadow from the gasometer creeps on; a slow,
    irrevocable flood.
It leaves behind the lilac, the bindweed, the sweet-scented
    camomiles.

Juggling in the Crematorium

Let's get the balance right.
No man's thoughts are heavier
than the ashes, waiting to be collected later.

Stepfather

I cannot pick him out the air,
he is not there;

nor out the soil,
the worm was not his style.

I cannot pick him out the fire,
there's not a cinder's worth left.

So why do I still feel bereft
when no love was lost?

Perhaps for what might have been
had he not been.

In the coffin he seems a replica,
a terrible dummy,

still wreaking havoc,
still beating up the living.

The Nightlight

For a year or more the nightlight stood on my bedside table.
Four inches high, owl-shaped.
With its bubbly, cream-coloured surface
And its two plastic halves joined by blobs of glue,
It was my childhood totem, my security.
How ferociously it glowed in the dark!
I snuggled down, not knowing there would never be
A time of such trust again.
Beyond the bedroom door adults stood guard,
Their presence an extra guarantee
That warded off so many different kinds of bogeymen.
But now I am back in the dark again.
The adults are gone.
Beyond the bedroom door is only the lack of them,
And there is no need of a bedside lamp to see
There is no bogeyman, bar one.
It's taken so long for him to cross the room.
Though truth is, he was never really gone.
No matter how many lights I put on
He was always there. From childhood to middle-age
He inched his way across the room unseen.
And now his fingers creep into me, into the cavities where
The heart rots and the blood sloshes about,
The bogeyman reaches to put out the nightlight.

An Incident

And when a child who has been sitting at a window
goes solemnly into another room and says
that he has seen an angel falling from Heaven,
who gets up to look? Who asks, 'Where?'
or, 'Is it hurt?' or says, 'How terrible!'

No, something has been drained from the adult heart.
Belief in the miraculous closes down
and that child's observation shrinks to a footnote,
an anecdote to be repeated in the future
when the dying hands of adults flick through albums.

How absurd, how comical then, that poor angel
bleeding among the winter marigolds. How monstrous
that it is dismissed so lightly, its memory gone,
the golden dust from those poor shattered wings
scattered over a suburban garden.

Ward Sixteen

At 2 a.m. last night, beyond the opaque doors of the hospital
  ward
in which I kept vigil, a glow appeared.
The duty nurse, bent over her reports, noticed nothing.
There was no sound other than the wheeze and creak of
  human wreckage,
of souls adrift in a drugged sleep, clinging still to bodies
  washed
by tidal-waves of pain.

There was no other light
but the low-watted bulb on the nurse's table.
The ward-door had not opened,
yet that glow entered,
pouring through the substance of the door
as if no barrier existed.

I thought it was my tiredness,
my own grief at an oncoming separation
that had caused a trick of light, a freak hallucination.
But the glow persisted. Drifting towards me
it flowed through the beds themselves,
and as it searched among the patients
it took shape, and I froze in awe.

It had become a creature, seven foot tall, hunched and radiant,
its golden skin the texture of a moth's wing.
It had come, breaking through the thin crust
that separates the mind from angels.
And by its light I saw how,
through the minute cracks in the surface of the hospital walls,
the horror of dying like liquid spilt.

Unaware of me, as if it were I who was insubstantial,
it crouched beside the bed in which my mother was lying
and stretching out a hand towards her
brushed all the hours of her life aside.

Under thin lids her eyes moved,
And though from that befuddled cocoon in which physical
     time was trapped
there came no final leavetaking,
something beyond doubt eased the terror
that came and went with each breath,
that came and went, then went,
and was gone forever.

How normal the ward seemed a moment later.
Beyond the opaque doors a solitary light-bulb glowed.
The duty-nurse yawned, not in the least distracted.

Ebb Tide and the Sparrow

My tongue has forgotten how to say
what my heart longs to say, and now
you will never hear it said.

Solitary one,
you are out on your own,
your pillow a rock in nothingness.

No borders,
no landfalls any more.
You are dissolving into my love for you.

Outside the window
a tiny bird is singing
a lament small as a seed.

The Khardoma

I went back to the basement café where so much time was spent so long ago. On the radio the Beatles were playing.

Brad came down the stairs in his absurdly old-fashioned suit and sat beside me. Pat followed, aloof as usual, and I felt so clumsy and loved her as ever I did.

Then Tasker joined us, hunched and manic in his ripped overcoat, his pockets stuffed with poems. Tim and Alice were with him. She'd just shoplifted The Whitsun Weddings.

Then Ajax, senior amongst us, with his moon-crater face and his first beard, sat down and nodded.

Since I last saw them I've learned so little.
Brad, Pat, Tasker, Ajax, Tim, Alice and all the others,
They come bobbing up on the currents that flow through
      memory,
Ahead of them still, the journeys they will never take,
The leaps of faith that will fail.
Armed with knowledge of the years to come
I sit among them, a ghost from their future.
Yet what could I tell them now, what could I say?
That one by one we would come to the end of
      transformations?
That we would become experts in forgetting?

In the Dark

Youth was over, it was gone,
It drifted out the skeleton.
It left its baggage but took away
Unquestioning immortality;
And all the buffers that had stood
Between the worm, the grave and me,
Faded imperceptibly,
And fear of the oncoming dark
So fogged up my mind that I
Forgot that the dark might pass by.

Ghost Ship

Dear ghost ship,
since you left this port,
your young crew hot with longings,
their semen hardly dry on women's lips,
the years have shrunk to a single
fleck-foamed wave;
the one who fathered me,
long dead.

Though there is a harbour into which
it is best never to find the way,
a sea-route it is best
never to follow,
fate and chance meetings will always
undo reason.
It is the seal's breath
melts the ice floe,
the flip of a gull's wing
changes the wind's course.

Five Down

She has closed her ears to the moth's weeping,
To the shadow's lament.

Her hands have abandoned the feel of cloth,
Her tongue has let go of tasting.

She has turned a blind eye to the darkness.

The scent of flowers rising from under a burden of rain
Has nowhere to go.

2

between harbours

These Boys Have Never Really Grown into Men

These boys have never really grown into men,
despite their disguises, despite their adult ways,
their sophistication, the camouflage of their kindly smiles.
They are still up to their old tricks,
still at the wing-plucking stage. Only now
their prey answers to women's names.
And the girls, likewise, despite their disguises,
despite their adult ways, their camouflage of need,
still twist love till its failure seems not of their making;
something grotesque migrates hourly
between our different needs,
and is in us all like a poison.
How strange I've not understood so clearly before
how liars and misers, the cruel and the arrogant
lie down and make love like all others,
how nothing is ever as expected, nothing is ever as stated.
Behind doors and windows nothing is ever as wanted.
The good have no monopoly on love.
All drink from it. All wear its absence like a shroud.

The Word

I did not know the workings of her mind;
Only that, from time to time in sleep,
She would let slip a single word,
One that, if heard, might have unlocked
Part of her awkwardness,
Her holding back.

She would curl up beside me in the bed
And I would strain to catch that word she said,
Though hearing it was something I had begun to dread.
It was mumbled; full of distress.
Muted by the thickness of her sleep,
How could a single word make her weep?

Too often and too obsessively I asked, but she
Was unable to explain what tormented her and I
Was unable to admit as to why
I wished so much to know,
And would not let my inquisition go.
Long after she had gone the mystery of that word lived on,

And it's only lately that I have come to understand
Why I could not hear what it was she said:
I did not listen for her sake, but for my own.
I did not listen out of love,
But out of fear –
And that alone is why I could not hear.

And now perhaps elsewhere, in her own or in another's bed
Someone with wiser ears than mine
Will have understood what it was she said,
And perhaps because of this
She will have let that word go.

It is something I will never know.

Don't Ask

Tell me, love, what were you thinking of?

I was thinking how there are certain times of the night
when the dead wipe the frost from their souls and weep.

Of nothing simpler?

Of a courtyard I once visited, and of a woman
standing beside a statue covered in snow.

Of no one else? No one nearer?

She was so beautiful,
Had she been made of nettles I'd have wanted her.

Why think of her now, at this moment?

Because I am still mixing the ashes of the dead and of dead
    obsessions.

Why answer me like this?

Because I am bankrupt of small comforts, of small deceits.
Because we two are new, and without history,
And treasonous memory sleeps in so many beds.

Survivor

Coming out of the storm it surprised us,
A survivor, alighting on a snapped branch,
Its wings still with their blue, crocus-coloured dust;
If only we'd had its luck
Coming out of our own storm, flightless now.

Her Coldness Explained

She said no man had ever hurt her,
She, who beside me like a statue lay.
And she would have me believe her heart
Was cold, and like a statue made of clay.

What? What did she say?
No man had ever hurt her?
She is so wrong.
Through her dreams her father walks night-long.

What I Need for the Present

Thanks, but please take back
the trinket box, the picture
made from butterfly wings and
the crystal glass.

Please take back the books,
the postcards, the beeswax candles,
the potted plant, the Hockney print
and the expensive pen.

Ungracious of me to say it, but
so many gifts that are given
are given in lieu of what
cannot be given.

Ungracious to say it, but
wherever I move in this room
it's not these gifts I see, but your absence
that accumulates on them like dust.

Forgive me. Your intentions
were so very kind, but here's
your box of fetters back. It's not
what I need for the present.

The Sick Equation

In school I learned that one and one made two,
It could have been engraved in stone,
An absolute I could not question or refute.
But at home, sweet home, that sum was open to dispute –
In that raw cocoon of parental hate is where
I learned that one and one stayed one and one.
What's more, because all that household's anger and its pain
Stung more than any teacher's cane
I came to believe how it was best
That one remained one,
For by becoming two, one at least would suffer so.

Believing this I threw away so many gifts –
I never let love stay long enough to take root,
But thinking myself of too little worth
I crushed all its messengers.

I grew – or did not grow –
And kept my head down low,
And drifted with the crowd,
One among the many whose dreams of flight
Weighed down the soul,
And kept it down,
Because to the flightless
The dream of flight's an anguish.

I stayed apart, stayed one,
Claiming separateness was out of choice,
And at every wedding ceremony I saw
The shadow of that albatross – divorce –
Fall over groom and bride,
And I took small comfort in believing that, to some degree
They too still harboured dreams of flying free.

I was wrong of course,
Just as those who brought me up were wrong.
It's absurd to believe all others are as damaged as ourselves,
And however late on, I am better off for knowing now
That given love, by taking love all can in time refute
The lesson that our parents taught,
And in their sick equation not stay caught.

The Recognition

In your late sixties now, older,
Likely to be alive somewhere, looking into mirrors still,
Or dead, with all things accounted for and put aside.
Decades have passed since I last thought of you
Yet it is only tonight that, finally, I understand you,
Realize how you must have felt
Lying beside me in that long-gone room,
The bark of a dog, the rattle of freight
On the world's muted periphery.
Twice my age then, half a lifetime beyond my reach,
Such a weight of knowledge separated flesh from flesh,
And amongst all that was mutual
Nothing could be equal.
Only tonight do I recognize the bleakness,
The sadness that overwhelmed you
And sent you hurrying back
To the safe harbour of your peers.
It invades me now as I stare at this woman,
So new and vulnerable beside me,
And wonder if, half a lifetime hence,
She too might feel such thoughts about me.

Dear Thief

You dress in silence
And tiptoe down the stairs
Never to return to this bed,
Still hot with longings.
It's six in the morning.
The bed creaks and clinks
Like an oven cooling.

Dear thief, I wonder if you realize
What it is you have stolen?

47

An Obsession

There are so many well-rehearsed farewells that have gone
      unsaid,
So many partings planned in the mind that the heart
Has not had the courage to follow through,
Although it knows, clairvoyant that it is,
The future holds no trace of you.
First it was your intelligence I loved,
Desire followed.
Your mouth blew the monotony of years aside.
I loved you first without expectation,
But then buckled under the weight
Of absurd hope. I loved you with a passion that lost its way
And became a sickness. Such was my obsession
I mistook your fear for coolness, forgetting
How this late on there are no new beginnings without
      betrayal.
I loved the tiredness of your breasts,
The softness of your stomach;
I was overawed by how all your adult life
Blood and milk have flowed endlessly from you.
You became my addiction, an obsession
Cured only by withdrawal.
Whenever I tried to break free of you
Timid reason was unravelled by love.

So many partings in the mind the heart
Has not had the courage to follow through.
God knows I tried, but in the darkness in which
Your body was another darkness,
Your mouth expertly stopped my questions,
Sabotaged the night's small vocabulary,
Sought to avoid all further duplicity.

The Wife

Absurdly, she thought Love was there for the taking,
Something gentle at her beck and call,
She thought it was her due, her given right;
That at her bidding Love would come submitting.
Then other needs took precedence,
For years she put all thought of it aside.
A dull husband, two kids, the house –
Like many others she made a compromise.
The slow drift to separate beds
Went by most unrecognized.
Then, long delayed by its other battles,
Unbidden and with a roaring arrogance Love came,
And she caught up in its chaos and its flame
Found her needs and Love's were not the same.

Hooks

In the middle of the night we finally turned to each other
and like sleepwalkers whose sleep had suddenly ended
wondered how we came to be lying together,
there in that strange room
where our clothes hung over chairs and on hooks,
and had about them the look
of things impatient to be going.

April Morning Walk

So many of those girls I longed for are gone now,
Gone to ash that skin so inexpertly kissed,
Those stomachs I was hot for, gone beyond diaries into flames.
When the years tore up their surface beauty and threw it away
Like the bright wrappings on a parcel
What was left was what links all the breathing world, an
    empathy,
The buried knowledge of our going.
It's so easy to forget how the years have poured away
And taken out of sequence and before their time
So many who deserved longer on this lush earth.

Along the streets in which I walked with them
The horse chestnut leaves are opening like Chinese fans.
The dawn's clear light varnishes houses and gardens
And freezes forever under its glittering surface
So much half-remembered anguish.

Second Act

The maps and timetables are on the mantelpiece.
The 'Sold' sign's gone up outside.
Most things are auctioned off.
It's dark already.
Someone you left long ago
Phones to say goodbye.

Waiting

It is far too late in the night to call you.
It is far too early in the morning for you to call.
We pace about, absurdly considerate.
Tell me, at what point did love become
The prisoner of schedules kept by shopkeepers?

Our Lives Had Grown so Empty

Remember the hibiscus we planted last spring?
Well, it flowered.
There is no other news.

3

inessential things

Inessential Things

What do cats remember of days?

They remember the ways in from the cold,
The warmest spot, the place of food.
They remember the places of pain, their enemies,
the irritation of birds, the warm fumes of the soil,
the usefulness of dust.
They remember the creak of a bed, the sound
of their owner's footsteps,
the taste of fish, the loveliness of cream.
Cats remember what is essential of days.
Letting all other memories go as of no worth
they sleep sounder than we,
whose hearts break remembering so many
inessential things.

The Minister for Exams

When I was a child I sat an exam.
The test was so simple
There was no way I could fail.

Q1. Describe the taste of the moon.

It tastes like Creation I wrote,
it has the flavour of starlight.

Q2. What colour is Love?

Love is the colour of the water a man
lost in the desert finds, I wrote.

Q3. Why do snowflakes melt?

I wrote, they melt because they fall
onto the warm tongue of God.

There were other questions.
They were as simple.

I described the grief of Adam when he was expelled from Eden.
I wrote down the exact weight of an elephant's dream.

Yet today, many years later,
for my living I sweep the streets
or clean out the toilets of the fat hotels.

Why? Because constantly I failed my exams.
Why? Well, let me set a test.

Q1. How large is a child's imagination?
Q2. How shallow is the soul of the Minister for Exams?

Tina's Flight

Some roads look as if they might go on forever
The way they twist and weave from place to place,
And others seem not really roads at all,
But runways sliced off from Earth and built
To launch us up, and off to Heaven.
I last saw you on such a road, your direction
Narrowed to harrowing certainties.
Head down, eyes peering from under a blonde fringe,
Arms held out steady like wings,
Your short future long diagnosed
You prepared to speed towards the sliced-off horizon,
And launch yourself Heavenward.
Gone now, you've left behind
A slowly dispersing trail of years.
I raise a glass of wine to a summer cloud,
To a child's balloon on its maiden voyage,
To your last signature scrawled on the sky's
Far-off, damson-coloured nothingness.

Devilment

He knows for certain there is no afterlife.
God came in a ring of frost-rimmed light and told him so.
He did not understand the meaning of God's joke,
But wave after wave of delight
Passed through him as God spoke.

Why Things Remained the Same

They change their sky, not their soul, who run across the sea
— HORACE

I kept on wanting to change.
I wanted to change my toys, my absurd balaclava,
my silly jumpers, my sensible shoes, my embarrassing coat,
my blotched exercise-books, my worn pen-nibs, my desk,
my lessons, my teachers,
the place in which I grew up, my cubbyhole of a bedroom,
the musky ex-army blankets, the mothballed cupboards,
the adults who perched over my life like crows.

It was not dissatisfaction alone, no,
something else made me wish to change
my awkwardness with girls, my first suit,
my spotty face, my hair, my age, my first sweetheart,
the borrowed room, the attic bedsit, the flat, the
    neighbourhood.
I wanted to change the bars in which I took refuge,
my friends, my ambitions, my possessions,
the books I'd written, the desk at which I sat,
my manner, my habits, my lovers, my house,
my standing among contemporaries.

I wished to change it all – my departure, my destination,
the schedules I'd set myself, the appointments I'd made,
the commitments I'd entered into.
I wanted to change the words I had spoken before crematoria
figured in the pages of diaries. I wanted so much to change,
but nothing changed except the need to change,
and day after day the excuses mounted,

    and they were so lightly made
I did not notice the weight of the baggage I carried,
nor of the indecisions I'd hauled from place to place
and year after year sought so ineffectually to abandon.

Poetry Lesson

Take these twenty-five words, for example.
Without the first line
Would rain falling on the tarpaulin
Covering the new grave
Be quite so poignant?

Waiting in Macedonia

In an empty hotel on the border
Of a country with no army,
The rooms shuttered, the pool
Given over to mosquitoes;
The Coca-Cola signs and travel adverts,
Kitsch exhibits fit for a museum now.
In the gardens of middle-class suburbs
Children play with useless banknotes,
Furtive adults bury petrol.
In town the pavement cafés
Bubble with rumours. Like clothes
That have been locked away too long
Old prejudices are aired. Someone
Mentions the Serbs. Someone
Mentions the Greeks. Someone
Mentions the Albanians. Someone
Mentions the Croats. Someone
Quotes Pushkin, '*Leave it alone:*
It is the Slavs' quarrel, a terrible family row
That fate decided long ago.' Someone
Slams the table in anger. Someone
Admits they don't understand.
Someone orders a coffee and a doughnut,
And whistles after a pretty girl who is passing.

Khartoum

The wind is carrying dust
From one place to another,
It carries its burden
Like an invisible donkey.
It cannot make up its mind
Where to stop, which street
To bury. Millimetre by millimetre,
Speck by speck, it encroaches
On all neighbourhoods,
Sneaks through the tall fences of compounds,
Covers kennels, spotlights, porches.
Fearless of the curfew
And of the passing jeeps, of the dog's bark
And the prehistoric tanks lounging
Beside sidings and bridges,
It carries its dust millennium
After millennium; the dust
Of palaces and army garrisons,
Of abandoned excavations, of people
No longer held together by blood.

Lockerbie

Yes, I remember the place –
The station. One dull afternoon
The train drew up there
Unexpectedly.

Before the town was reached
From the windows I saw
The usual picture-postcard scenery.
The sheep-cropped fields revealed

No hint of catastrophe.
A few passengers looked up,
And jolted from a Sunday doze
They saw the place's name and froze.

Opposite me a woman wept.
Some people came aboard,
And passed on the baton of their grief
To those who left. The place's name

Was not observed by all.
Noses stuck in books some read on
As car parks, new housing, dull fields,
Were quickly passed, then gone.

So Many Different Lengths of Time

Cuanto vive el hombre por fin? Vive mil dias o uno solo?
Una semana o varios siglos? Por cuanto tiempo muere el hombre?
Que quiere decir 'para siempre'?
Preocupado per este asunto me dedique a aclarar las cosas.
— PABLO NERUDA

How long is a man's life, finally?
Is it a thousand days, or only one?
One week, or a few centuries?
How long does a man's death last?
And what do we mean when we say, 'gone forever'?

Adrift in such preoccupations, we seek clarification.
We can go to the philosophers,
but they will grow tired of our questions.
We can go to the priests and the rabbis
but they might be too busy with administrations.

*   *   *

So, how long does a man live, finally?
And how much does he live while he lives?
We fret, and ask so many questions —
then when it comes to us
the answer is so simple.

70

A man lives for as long as we carry him inside us,
for as long as we carry the harvest of his dreams,
for as long as we ourselves live,
holding memories in common, a man lives.

His lover will carry his man's scent, his touch;
his children will carry the weight of his love.
One friend will carry his arguments,
another will hum his favourite tunes,
another will still share his terrors.

And the days will pass with baffled faces,
then the weeks, then the months,
then there will be a day when no question is asked,
and the knots of grief will loosen in the stomach,
and the puffed faces will calm.
And on that day he will not have ceased,
but will have ceased to be separated by death.
How long does a man live, finally?

A man lives so many different lengths of time.

Drinking to the Muse

After the first drink the Muse takes notice.
After the second she's on your side.
With the third she's showing you the world
As it ought to be, benign, rose-hued,
And all is smiles and forgiveness.
Then with the fourth drink she grows impatient.
Her ears embarrassed by maudlin confessions
When the fifth releases an incoherent prayer
Of which she disapproves, you're abandoned
To the sixth, to the seventh, to the darkness again.

Circus Trick

Like a lion-tamer opening a lion's mouth
Someone feigning love
Is opening their heart to her.
It's an old circus trick.
That she should fall for it again and again.
Still astounds her.

Above her the tightrope is slippery with wounds.

The Mirror's Apprentice

Naïvely, I envied the simplicity of mirrors.
What had they to report other than what passed before them?
How could they not tell the truth?
I imagined mirrors saw clearly, coldly,
Uninfluenced by any notion of ugliness or beauty,
And I longed for once to see the world
The way a mirror sees it.
And so it was I became a mirror's apprentice.
I sneaked into rooms side-on to catch them off-guard.
I sat in corners and studied their genius.
I realized how, in millions upon millions of houses,
In palaces and army garrisons, in churches and towerblocks,
In railway stations and in endless sad cubicles,
Mirrors paid the living no special attention.
I began to see as a mirror sees.
I saw how dust accumulates in the folds of curtains,
I saw the colour fading from fabrics.
A vase of flowers grew old before my eyes,
Each separate speck of pollen crumbled and fell
And a breeze, imperceptible to human skin,
Blew it away.
I dreamed a mirror's dream,
I became a still pool reflecting the pterodactyl's flight,
Became a particle of light on a wasp's antenna.

How absurd it was to have considered them inanimate,
To have imagined they reported on only what passed before
them.
My apprenticeship over,
I took up residence on the far side of mirrors.
And in that mummified light,
Among the dust of ancient reflections,
I discovered their slow mortality.
Like lungs that have held breath but can no longer hold it
Their quicksilver backing flakes away.
They're as vulnerable as all they reflect,
Whether it's a face in a glass,
Or stars trapped like crustacea in a satellite's bowl
As it trawls the rim of Heaven.

Garden Lore

Who will take care of this garden, who will nurture it?

'I will,' said January.
'I will anchor it to the earth with snowdrops.
I will give it my stone, the garnet.'

'It is mine,' said February.
'I will feed it the memory of all that grows.
I will welcome it with amethyst and primrose.'

'I will coax it with bloodstone and daffodil,' said March.
'Like a boxer battered by winter
I will lift myself from the frosty canvas of the earth to
    welcome it.'

'With diamond and daisy I will seduce it.
I will soak it in shower after shower,' said April.
'In the yawny earth its seeds will riot.'

'I will make it dizzy with emeralds
and the fumes of the hawthorn,' said May.
'It will know of nothing but play.'

'And I will adorn it with a necklace
of honeysuckle and ruby,' said June.
'It will dance to my languid tune.'

'I will contain it,' said July.
'I will handcuff it with briar and chrysolite,
drug it with the scent of roses.'

August spoke from the garden's stillness.
'I will weep layer upon layer of sardonyx.
I will teach it the brevity of poppies.'

'When its bones begin to creak
I will cure it with aster and opal,'
promised September.

'I will guide it towards sleep with the cold light of sapphires;
For its lullaby I will provide the swan song of dahlias,'
said October.

'Under the weight of dead chrysanthemums I will bury it,'
said November. 'I will give it a headstone of topaz,
a rosary of berries.'

'And I will guard its sleep,' said December.
'On a pillow of moonstone
It will dream of holly and the coming snowdrop.'

In Perspective

Across the rich earth, the fat orchards, the fields I hardly knew,
Happiness came bounding towards me,
A hungry puppy, mistaking me for its master.

Fine, I thought, let the mistake stand,
The bones in my pockets
Have weighed me down long enough.

Happiness like sorrow, needs to be fed.

Full Circle World

Good morning dear world,
So briefly known.
In flashes only seen,
So often missed
By eyes so self-obsessed.
Good morning dear earth,
With your clouds like flags unfurled
And your sun that walks on beams of frost
And lights all we thought lost.
Good morning dear mist,
Dear floating lakes of light through which
The numbed bee and its cargo sails.
Good morning dear sky,
Dear scented woven threads of air
That blow away despair
From this world so briefly known,
In flashes only seen,
So often missed
By eyes so self-obsessed.
Good morning dear world.

Into the Blue

They remind me of children
With a faith so simple,
With a faith so gigantic.

As a delighted child leaps
Into its parents' arms
Trusting it will be caught,

So the dolphin leaps
Into the blue arms of the sky,
Trusting it will fall back unharmed.

Sea Saw

There was a man who sold regrets by the ounce. He had a little shop tucked away behind a busy main street not far from the docks. Sailors landing from long voyages would make pilgrimages to his shop, for their hearts were so cauterized by salt they could feel nothing of their own accord. They would buy phials containing the scents of places they would never visit again, and some would have their arms tattooed with the sighs of love-sick girls.

The Brackets

I look down the contents list at the poets' names –
de la Mare (1873–1956)
Farjeon (1881–1965)
Graves (1895–1985)

I look down the list then stop,
Then look up again at one sandwiched between
These benign octogenarians –
Owen (1893–1918)

At first it seems unfair,
Twenty-five, then gone. Hard to believe
I drank beneath the stars with one
Who crouched beneath the light from flack with him,

Or that in my teens I'd briefly met
A woman who had known
His beauty and his awkwardness.
Now she too is bone.

No longer the youngest on the contents list
The names of friends crop up.
Some are gone –
Tumour-ridden, the brackets close in.

They drop against the ends of names,
Not orderly, but any old how.
Henri, Mitchell, McGough – watch it mates,
The brackets, any day now.

Carol Shields

Mary Swann

'A brilliant literary mystery. Read it'   *Independent on Sunday*

'One of the best novels I have read this year. It's deft, funny, poignant, surprising, and beautifully shaped'   Margaret Atwood

Mary Swann, a latter-day Emily Dickinson, submitted a paper bag full of poems to newspaper editor Frederic Cruzzi mere hours before her husband hacked her to pieces. How could someone who led such a dull, sheltered life produce these works of genius? Four very different people search for the elusive answer in this teasing, inventive and beautiful narrative . . .

'A very good novel , alive in every sense: formally ingenious and inventive, strikingly evocative of place, of character, of the world of things, capable of both comedy and tenderness, and above all beautifully written'   *London Review of Books*

'Clearly the work of an experienced and skilful writer . . . This is not only a first rate read, it is also sophisticated and ingeniously crafted'   *Listener*

flamingo

Jane Smiley

A Thousand Acres

**Winner of the Pulitzer Prize for Fiction
and the
US National Book Critics' Circle Award**

Larry Cook's farm is the largest in Zebulon County, Iowa, and a tribute to his hard work and single-mindedness. Proud and possessive, his sudden decision to retire and hand over the farm to his three daughters, is disarmingly uncharacteristic. Ginny and Rose, the two eldest, are startled yet eager to accept, but Caroline, the youngest daughter, has misgivings. Immediately, her father cuts her out.

In *A Thousand Acres* Jane Smiley transposes the *King Lear* story to the modern day, and in so doing at once illuminates Shakespeare's original and subtly transforms it.

'A near-miraculous success'   *Washington Post*

'Commanding, mythic, beautiful'   *Boston Globe*

'Powerful, poignant, intimate and involving'   *New York Times*

'While Smiley has written beautifully about families in all of her preceding books, her latest effort is her best; a family portrait that is also a near-epic investigation into the broad landscape, the thousand dark acres, of the human heart. The book has all the stark brutality of a Shakespearean tragedy.'   *Washington Post*

flamingo

Brian Moore

Cold Heaven

'Compulsive reading . . . Brian Moore writes like a dream.'
Guardian

On holiday in the south of France, Dr Alex Davenport is
caught up in a fatal accident at sea. His wife, Marie, suddenly
finds herself in the bitterly ironic position of a woman who
has lost the husband she had been planning to leave for
another man – she had just been waiting for the right time to
tell him. A day later, however, she is summoned to the hospital
to be told that his body has disappeared from the morgue.
Returning in confusion to the hotel, she then discovers that
his clothes, passport and plane ticket have also gone . . .

Moving from the Riviera to the coast of California, *Cold
Heaven* is a compulsive and hypnotic tale of the bizarre, the
inexplicable, the supernatural and the eccentricities of every-
day life.

'Striking and strange, *Cold Heaven* is told with the panicky
sense of urgency at which Moore excels.'   *Observer*

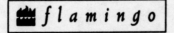

Random Acts of Senseless Violence
Jack Womack

'If you dropped the characters from *Neuromancer* into
Womack's Manhatten, they'd fall down screaming and
have nervous breakdowns' WILLIAM GIBSON

It's just a little later than now and Lola Hart is writing her
life in a diary. She's a nice middle-class girl on the verge of
her teens who schools at the calm end of town.

A normal, happy girl.

But in a disintegrating New York she is a dying breed. War
is breaking out on Long Island, the army boys are flame-
throwing the streets, five Presidents have been assassinated
in a year. No one notices any more.

Soon Lola and her family must move over to the Lower
East Side - Loisaida - to the Pit and the new language and
violence of the streets.

The metamorphosis of the nice Lola Hart into the new
model Lola has begun . . .

'Womack astounds and entertains'   *Publishers Weekly*

ISBN 0 586 21320 1

Random Acts of Senseless Violence

Jack Womack